RABBIT SEEDS

WRITTEN AND ILLUSTRATED BY
BIJOU LE TORD

A PICTURE YEARLING BOOK

Published by
Dell Publishing
a division of
Bantam Doubleday Dell Publishing Group, Inc.
666 Fifth Avenue
New York, New York 10103

ISBN: 0-440-40767-2

Reprinted by arrangement with the author

Printed in the United States of America

March 1993

10 9 8 7 6 5 4 3 2 1
DAN

TO FRÉDÉRIQUE

When the ice and snow are gone,

and the sun warms up the earth,

a gardener begins his work.

He takes out his wheelbarrow,
a spade, a rake, and a hoe.

He tills his garden,
breaks up clumps
of heavy soil,

rakes away stones,
and cleans out
the winter mulch.

He plans where to sow
each new crop,

draws a tight string
to guide his furrows
and the tiny seeds.

He labels carrots,
lettuces, onions,
and closes up
the fragile rows.

His sweet peas
will climb a fence.
His marigolds
will keep away beetles.

When the day cools,
he waters his seeds.

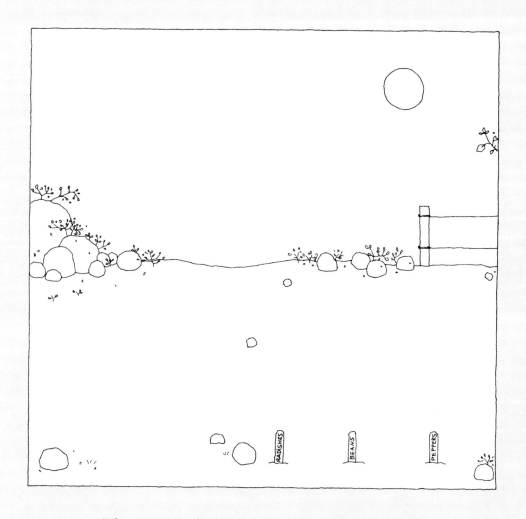

The sun and the earth begin their work.

He patiently waits,

and watches for a first
ripple or a crack
on the ground.

He patiently sits,

until the first seedlings shoot up.

Young tomato plants
need the open air,

weeds grow fast,
shadowing
new sprouts.

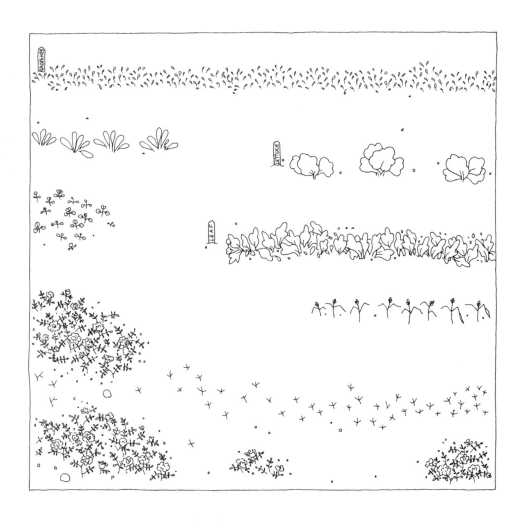

Baby lettuces push up,
buds unfold,
radishes need thinning.

Early peas wear pink,
carrots are tender,
parsley is ready.

He digs out
tender new potatoes,

and sets greens,
sweet peppers, and peas
in small crates.

A melon
feels heavy,
when it is just ripe.

Cauliflowers
and artichokes
are for sale.

When leaves turn yellow,

just before the ground freezes,

a gardener puts away his tools.

His work is done.

The sun and leaves
will protect his garden
all winter.